SHAKING
FOR
SHIFTING

Apostle
Mike O. Ibitoye

Understanding the phases and seasons of life

SHAKING FOR SHIFTING

All Scriptural quotations are taken from the King James Version (KJV) of the Bible

Forward enquiries to:

WINNING IN LIFE INTERNATIONAL MINISTRIES
Tel: +27 (0) 78 978 7816 (South Africa).
+234 (0) 703 924 9322 (Nigeria)
E-mail: michaelibitoye@gmail.com
Website: winninginlifeint.co.za

TABLE OF CONTENTS

Dedication

This book is dedicated to my late wife Pastor Nene Ibitoye. We started it together and she edited the first six chapters. She stood by me all through my ministerial journeys both home and abroad till death. Your memories are evergreen in my heart. I will continue from where you left. I love you even in death.

Acknowledgment

I will always thank the Almighty God who is my source of inspiration. I am today and all I will become, I owe it to Him.

I specially thank our church members who have encouraged me and my family in their little way to ensure the church is standing and moving when lots of members abandoned us. Thanks to KC and Pamela Naidoo for being a son and daughter that understand the heart of a father, you are forever blessed in Jesus name. Thanks to Kennedy Ekpah for sharing in our family pains and going the extra mile to serve us, you will not lose your reward. Many thanks to Kuda Gwadzoka for your financial commitment to the church, you will never lack in Jesus name.

I want to appreciate Mrs Blessing Ajetunmobi of Bronny Concept, Nigeria Company for arranging this book. May God enlarge your coast.

My thanks specially go to my late wife Nene Ibitoye and children Mojisola, Oluwadamilola and Olamide for the pains and joy they have been through with me in foreign mission. We shall continue the mission as there are more territories to conquer

Introduction

This book is written to share my wealth of experience in life and ministry.

I stepped out into full time ministry 1989 at a tender age of 20 having grown up in my late father's church. I wanted to serve under the church my father founded but the church leadership did not give me the opportunity to do so. My mother and siblings had to leave the church to face the realm of the unknown. But right deep in my heart, I knew I was called to work for God. My parents dedicated me to the altar while I was a baby to work for God. That's why the God of the altar has refused to leave me alone because there is a covenant on my life.

I have gone through some experiences in ministry which have shaped my life. I have seen the good, bad, and the ugly sides of ministry.

My first experience was when I was picked from the bible school in 1989 by my first mentor and Father Rev Collins Boussa. He brought me to his church. It was there I learnt the rudiments of ministry. He commissioned me into ministry. I served him for 6years until I had a leading to move to another city. There was a calling on my life which I was trying to discover more and expressed to my generation. I then moved to another church where I served for another two years 1994 - 1996 (Grace Fellowship Centre)

I went into church planting in 1996 with the aim of expressing God's call and mandate. I ran the church for five years. I couldn't continue because of the challenges I went through as a youth. I then called my young members to go look for another church to attend. The good news is that all those members are pastors today.

In June 21 2001, God gave me the vision I have been craving for. It was an outreach mandate of raising people from the bottom to the top and empowering them to discover and harness their potentials in order to live winning always in life. I got the name by revelation (Winning in Life International). I set out with a team of ministers who have been impacted by my life and ministry. We kept holding seminars, conferences and summit at various churches and halls. While running the outreach, I joined a church to serve as a music minister and later branch pastor (The Fountain of Life Church, now The Still Waters Church)

I had great success in outreach ministry. Few years later in 2005, I went into church planting again. I planted a church and run it for one year before I received the mandate from God in 2006 to reach out to South Africa as my next phase of assignment. While in South Africa, I kept on with Winning in Life conferences and lives were touched and imparted too.

Ministry Shakings

I had an immigration problem in 2008 which led to me being deported from South Africa back to Nigeria. It was one of the greatest shakings of my life. I left my wife and children in South Africa. Five months later, I came back to South Africa to my family. I then planted our present church, The Winning Life Church in Cape Town in 2010. I have battled to grow this church by faith. The church grew after few years drawing people of different colours and nations. We have seen shakings. We have tried to move from the community we are but never been able. People have left the church while others kept coming. Looking at the inputs we have put in, I began to ask God why we are going through all manner of shakings. As I sought the face of God, he gave me the answer. He has given me an apostolic ministry, to reach out to the Body of Christ, not to sit down at the four walls of the church. He is the builder of the church. What I noticed through my experience of pastoring is this: Whenever I go on apostolic outreach, the church grows, but when I come back and stay for months, the church begins to struggle to grow.

The Shifting

The reason for all the shakings is because I needed to shift in mind set, operation, message, and organisation. God instructed me to empower leaders for the next phase and focus more on my apostolic assignment of church planting, leadership empowerments, and ministry outreach to the Body of Christ.

The Action

It has taken me almost thirty years of full time ministry to shift and step fully into the apostolic mandate that God has called me into.

Are you a leader going through severe shakings, God is about to shift you in order to align you into the assignment He has for you.

As you go through the pages of this book, may God open your understanding into your assignment in Jesus name. God bless you.

Shaking for shifting

SHAKING IS PART OF LIFE

As an eagle stirreth up her nest, fluttereth over her young, spreadeth abroad her wings, taketh them, beareth them on her wings: So the LORD alone did lead him, and there was no strange god with him"
Deut 32:11-12.

Stirring is necessary if the eaglet in the nest must know how to soar. The mother eagle has to stir the nest to make the eaglet uncomfortable because they have come to maturity to soar. The same way, God rocks our comfort zone to enable us to understand that we are in a new season and must move to the next dimension.

Stirring is also shaking. If it seems you are going through shaking, God is just stirring your nest for the next move. God does nothing without purpose. Nothing happens without His knowledge and permission. He has something in mind He wants to pass across to you.

Shaking is common to ministry, business and every career in life. When you have not experienced shaking in your assignment, watch it, you might just be on the wrong path and you will remain immature. It is shaking that breaks, moulds, makes, and transforms you into the person you are meant to be.

Shaking brings direction and instructions; it gives you a clear vision of your mandate. Shaking reveals your real identity. It brings out your true colour. You will not know your true disciples and followers as a pastor until you experience some shakings.

Your true friends are revealed in the season of shaking. Just like the paralyzed man in Luke 4. I am sure he was left on his own when he was at the shakings of life, but four good friends stood with him and helped him to his place of miracles.

When you are too comfortable in your assignment, shaking must surely come to fire up your zeal to pursue once more.

God allows enemies to shake you so you can rise up to your responsibility. In politics, there must be an opposition party, this helps brings out your potential drive to make a difference.

There is something about shaking. If there is no shaking, there will be no shifting. The early church were in one place, without fulfilling the great commission, but God allowed a great shaking to them that brought about the spreading of the gospel to the uttermost part of the world.

The church today is going through shaking because she has lost her focus. Instead of building disciples for the kingdom, we are building them for ourselves. We focus on raising buildings more than kingdom minded people. God will allow policies and agents of the enemy to shake the church so she can get back to purpose.

Shaking prunes out the chaff from you and brings out your true shape from where you begin to manifest the real 'you' God has designed for His purpose.

There is a purpose for every shaking. You may be complaining because you lack understanding. I pray that God opens you up to spiritual understanding of His purpose and counsel.

Chapter 2

THE EAGLES STIRRING

"As an eagle stirreth up her nest, fluttereth over her young, spreadeth abroad her wings, taketh them, beareth them on her wings: So the LORD alone did lead him" Deut 32:11-12.

We need to be stirred at all times at every level to grow into maturity and responsibility. God stirs His people like the mother eagle does to the eaglets in order to lead them to the place He has prepared for them. The believers are seen as the eagles.

"Ye have seen what I did unto the Egyptians, and how I bare you on eagles'

***wings, and brought you unto myself"
Exodus 9:4.***

The Eagle

The Eagle is among the falcon's family. They are the strongest amongst birds. They operate on a higher altitude and heights. As believers, we must not be satisfied with operations on the lower level. Our focus must be on things above (Col 3:1-3). When you operate on the heavenly places, you control the plain. Everything on the plain has no control over your life.

Their Homes

"Doth the eagle mount up at thy command, and make her nest on high? She dwelleth and abideth on the rock, upon the crag of the rock, and the strong place. From thence she seeketh the prey, and her eyes behold afar off" Job 39:27-30.

The Eagle dwells on top of the highest rock and strong places. So also we are encouraged to build our house on the rock for stability (Psalm 91:1-2). From the highest rock she sees her prey and goes into action.

The Training Process

The Eagle builds her nest in layers with lots of materials. The first layer is the thorns. Second layer is the hardwood. Third layer is palm leaves. Fourth layer is the wool. She lays her eggs on the wool for comfort. When the eggs are hatched, the eaglets grow up and get used to the wool. Then, the mother eagle removes the wool, leaving them on the third layer- the palm leaves. When they get used to the leaves, the mother eagle removed the leaves to the second layer- the hardwood. Here is when things look hard. After that, she removes the hardwood to the first layer - the thorns. This time, living becomes unbearable for the eaglets. The thorns choke them...then they cry out seeing their mother as very wicked

In the mind of the mother eagle, she is aiming at teaching them to grow up and fly on their own. Those uncomfortable experiences you are going through are the shakings of God to help you to maturity.

The real shaking

The mother eagle seeing the eaglets are getting used to the thorns, scatters the entire nest and throw them down from the high mountain into the sky. While the eaglets are falling from the top they are scared and scream for help. In that process, suddenly, the mother eagle spread her wings and picks them up back to the high rock. This she does several times until the eaglets understand that their mother wants them to fly and soar. Eventually, they spread out their wings themselves and began to soar on their own.

When things look so hard for you, it is God shaking and stirring your comfort zone for you to learn the lessons of life. He wants you to soar against and beyond the storms of life. It may seem as if you are falling, finished, dejected, abandoned, broken, shattered, and people are making mockery of you, don't worry, you are still in the hands of the Almighty God. He is teaching you some lessons of life that will make and mould you.

In the process of shaking, you develop stamina, muscles, knowledge, potentials, and experiences which help you to live in the next dimension and phase of your life. All my write-ups and teachings came from what I learnt in the process of my shakings in life. That's why I am original.

Friends, don't give up in life! Don't give in or bow down to pressures! Don't accept the alternatives; keep pressing on for the ultimate. Very soon you will declare like Job:

"But He knows the way that I take, when He has tried me, I shall come forth as gold" Job 3:10.

Shaking for shifting

Chapter 3

GOD'S PURPOSE FOR SHAKING

Shakings are natural to life and necessary for your flight. No shaking is without purpose. Let's see some of them.

1. To Bring Us Back to Himself

"Ye have seen what I did unto the Egyptians, and how I bare you on eagles' wings, and brought you unto myself" *Exodus 19:4.*

Most times we miss it and God allows shakings to bring us back to Divine purpose. There is one funny thing about God. He uses your enemy to afflict you in order to gain your attention, after that, He will turn back and deal with the enemy. He reminded the Israelites of what He did to the Egyptians in the Red Sea. The irony of it is that, He allowed the Egyptians to afflict them because they became too comfortable in Egypt. His intention was for them to possesses the land of Canaan

"And he said unto Abram, Know of a surety that thy seed shall be a stranger in a land that is not theirs, and shall serve them; and they shall afflict them four hundred years; And also that nation, whom they shall serve, will I judge: and afterward shall they come out with great substance" Gen15:13-14.

They were to spend four hundred years in Egypt, but they spent four hundred and thirty years (Extra thirty years). When you have overstayed your place of current assignment, you are getting out of the will of God, and He will allow shakings to get you on purpose. Please don't be out of tune with God.

2.   To Know The State Of Our Hearts

Love is not true until it is truly tested. Most of us confessed we love God, but God allows shakings to prove our love for Him. Imagine how many people have turned their backs on God.

"And thou shalt remember all the way which the LORD thy God led thee these forty years in the wilderness, to humble thee, and to prove thee, to know what was in thine heart, whether thou wouldest keep his commandments, or no. And he humbled thee, and suffered thee to hunger, and fed thee with manna, which thou knewest not, neither did thy fathers know; that he might make thee know that man doth not live by bread only, but by every word that proceedeth out of the mouth of the LORD doth man live." Deut 8:3-4.

Will you remain standing during shakings? Shakings humble us. It tells us that things cannot be rosy all the time (we can't live just by bread alone).

God also tested Abraham to sacrifice his only son and he passed the test. That was why he was called the friend of God. Will you pass God's test?

"And it came to pass after these things, that God did tempt Abraham, and said unto him, Abraham: and he said, Behold, here I am" Genesis 22:1.

"And he said, Lay not thine hand upon the lad, neither do thou anything unto him: for now I know that thou fearest God, seeing thou hast not withheld thy son, thine only son from me" Genesis 22:12.

If God tells you to release your valuable thing for Him like car, house, clothes, treasure etc, what will your response be? The test of true love is sacrifice. God is a God of sacrifice and He honours such that will act like Him.

3. To Produce Character in Us

"Now no chastening for the present seemeth to be joyous, but grievous: nevertheless afterward it yieldeth the peaceable fruit of righteousness unto them which are exercised thereby" Hebrews 12:11.

Chastisement is part of the shakings of God. The end product of it is the fruit of righteousness which is character. God uses shakings to shape and mould us so that His true life style will be seen in us. Do not despise the chastening of the Lord, (Heb 12:5) they are needed for us to grow into maturity. That is why God relates with us like the mother eagle does to the eaglets so they can take responsibility and meet up with the next generation of champions.

4. To Prosper His Children

"For thus saith the LORD of hosts; Yet once, it is a little while, and I will shake the heavens, and the earth, and the sea, and the dry land; And I will shake all nations, and

the desire of all nations shall come: and I will fill this house with glory, saith the LORD of hosts. The silver is mine, and the gold is mine, saith the LORD of hosts. The glory of this latter house shall be greater than of the former, saith the LORD of hosts: and in this place will I give peace, saith the LORD of hosts" Haggai 2:6-9

Some shakings are necessary to bring you into prosperity. God's intention is to cause His children to enjoy wealth transfer. He shakes heaven and earth to fill His house with glory. That glory is seen when silver and gold (prosperity) are released to advance His Kingdom.

He shook Egypt with famine, yet Joseph by Divine wisdom was in plenty (Genesis 41:50).

He caused famine to come in Israel, yet Elijah was fed by ravens, the widow, and the angel (1 Kings 17).

When there are shakings going on in nations, it looks grievous, but God will cause His children to enjoy supernatural supplies and not to rely on the arm of the flesh.

God stirred the nest like the Eagle to bring increase:

"As an eagle stirreth up her nest, fluttereth over her young, spreadeth abroad her wings, taketh them, beareth them on her wings: So the LORD alone did lead him, and there was no strange god with him. He made him ride on the high places of the earth, that he might eat the increase of the fields; and he made him to suck honey out of the rock, and oil out of the flinty rock;" *Deut 32:11-13.*

He made us to ride on the high places of the earth so that we eat the increase of the field, suck honey from the rock, and oil. This speaks of prosperity. Where things look so hard and rocky, that is where God leads His children to abundance.

Shakings bring us into a wealthy place:

"For thou, O God, hast proved us: thou hast tried us, as silver is tried. Thou broughtest us into the net; thou laidst affliction upon our loins. Thou hast caused men to ride over our heads; we went through fire and through water: but thou broughtest us out into a wealthy place" Psalms 66:10-12.

If the place you are right now will not help you fulfil God's purpose, God must shake you because you must move to the place called 'there'. If the eaglets are not shaken out of the nest by mother eagle, they will not soar to discover the vast opportunities in the sky and on the land. They will remain in the nest. It's time to grow up and go up.

5.   **To Renew Our Strength**
"Who satisfieth thy mouth with good things; so that thy youth is renewed like the eagles" Psalm 103:5

At old age, the eagles take vacation to the top of the mountains. From there, they pull out their old feathers and beaks. They stay up there for a long time feeding on honey until new feathers and beaks grow out again. Then they soar again. Shaking out the feathers brings out new ones.

Shaking is also like a vacation time where no one sees you again. It is your silent moment. You are going through some pruning. It is the time to wait upon God and seeking His face for the next move. This time, your will, emotions, agenda, pride, will be crushed in God's presence. When you come out again, waoh! It's a new you with new strength, vision and passion.

"But they that wait upon the LORD shall renew their strength; they shall mount up with wings as eagles; they shall run, and not be weary; and they shall walk, and not faint" Isaiah 40:31.

"But he knoweth the way that I take: when he hath tried me, I shall come forth as gold" *Job 23:10.*

You are coming out greater in a grand year in Jesus name.

Chapter 4

JONAH SHAKING EXPERIENCE

"But the LORD sent out a great wind into the sea, and there was a mighty tempest in the sea, so that the ship was like to be broken" Jonah 1:4.

I call this **'When God rocks your Boat'**
Jonah was a prophet sent by God on a mission to warn the people of Nineveh about their sins. But Jonah instead of obeying the instructions of God took a ship to a different direction (Tarshish).

It is not our idea or ambition that matters in fulfilling God's mission for our lives; it is the heavenly vision and mandate from God. God had a purpose in mind for sending Jonah to Nineveh. It can be for just one person. Your assignment may be to an unlikely place to reach just some few people. Obedience is very important in our walk with God. Where I am located may not be where I love, but if that is where God wants me to be per time, He will reward me according to my obedience.

What God did to Jonah

1.   He sent a great wind to the sea

Some storms are permitted by God to discipline you and bring you back to order and purpose. Jonah was out of the will of God.

God uses storms most times to get your attention. He allowed the bush to burn without being consumed so Moses could turn aside and get His attention. This becomes a shaking. The ship was shaken and almost broken to pieces.

Someone's disobedience can affect other's comfort. The consequence of a father's mistake and error can affect the children born and unborn. I am a living witness. My late father, a pastor, left his assignment to pursue other means of survival. He died in the process and we, the children had to suffer to grow and become who we are today.

Jonah fled from God's presence to Tarshish and hide in the lowest part of the ship. You cannot hide from God's presence.

David said in Psalm 139:7-10 ***"Whither shall I go from thy spirit? or whither shall I flee from thy presence? If I ascend up into heaven, thou art there: if I make my bed in hell, behold, thou art there. If I take the wings of the morning, and dwell in the uttermost parts of the sea; Even there shall thy hand lead me, and thy right hand shall hold me"***

The mariners were so scared of the storm. They threw all their belongings into the sea to lessen the storm, but there was no solution, until they prayed and casted lot, then the lot fell on Jonah. God will expose the cause of shaking in your life.

2.   Jonah was casted into the sea

Then the wind ceased. Some Jonahs in your life, family, business, and ministry must go for peace to come. The sea was another dimension of shaking. It is easier to be in a stormy ship than the sea. You can't breathe inside the sea, you will choke to death.

3.   God sent a Great Fish (Whale) To Swallow Jonah

"Now the LORD had prepared a great fish to swallow up Jonah. And Jonah was in the belly of the fish three days and three nights" Jonah 1:7

This is a higher dimension of shaking. Jonah moved from troubled ship, to the sea, then to the belly of the fish. This is too much for a man or child of God.

It was God that sent the storm and the fish. Don't conclude the life of someone who is going through shaking by the hands of God. Just allow God to finish His work in his life.

How did Jonah survive the fish belly for three days? Why is it that the digestive system of the fish couldn't crush Jonah? Let's move to the next chapter.

Chapter 5

WHY WAS JONAH NOT CONSUMED IN THE FISH BELLY?

We saw in the previous chapter the shaking that Jonah went through when he ran from God's instructions. The ship was troubled, he was thrown into the sea, and eventually, he was swallowed by a great fish sent by God. We face shaking often when we are not sensitive to God's instructions or when we are too busy to hear him. Why was Jonah not consumed?

1.   God was involved

When God shakes you, His intention is to remove all the dross in you and bring out the gold. You will see some people go through severe shaking and still bounce back. Some churches go through shaking and later come back stronger and better. The reason is because God was pruning some bad members away. God will shake off anyone that will hinder your journey of destiny just like He separated Lot from Abraham. Some shakings are necessary to reveal your true sons and daughters.

"We are troubled on every side, yet not distressed; we are perplexed, but not in despair; Persecuted, but not forsaken; cast down, but not destroyed; Always bearing about in the body the dying of the Lord Jesus, that the life also of Jesus might be made manifest in our body" 2 Cor 4:8-10.

Shaking allows us to submit to the Will of God. Jesus seeing what He would go through in the Garden of Gethsemane, prayed "...not my will but your will be done" Matthew 26:39. At the Garden of Eden, we lost our will to Satan through Adam. But at the Garden of

Gethsemane, our will was restored back to the Father though Christ.

The three Hebrew children (Shadrak, Meshak, and Abednego) went through the fire and came out unharmed, because God was involved. Daniel was was thrown into the Lion's den and came out unharmed because God was involved.

When God is involved in your shaking, no power can crush you, no death will take you, no situation can destroy you.

2.   The Mercies of God

It was of the Lord's mercies that Jonah was not consumed. Jonah was alive in the fish three days and nights: to nature this was impossible, but to the God of nature all things are possible. Jonah, by this miraculous preservation, was made a type of Christ as our blessed Lord himself declared in Matthew 12:40.

"It is of the LORD'S mercies that we are not consumed, because his compassions fail not. They are new every morning: great is thy faithfulness" Lamentation 3:22-23.

A song writer sang this song: 'Great is your mercy towards me, your loving kindness towards me. Your tender mercies I see, day after day. Forever faithful towards me, always providing for me, great is your mercy toward me, great is your grace'

David said in Psalm 124:1-8 *"If it had not been the LORD who was on our side, now may Israel say; If it had not been the LORD who was on our side, when men rose up against us: Then they had swallowed us up quick, when their wrath was kindled against us: Then the waters had overwhelmed us, the stream had gone over our soul: Then the proud waters had gone over our soul. Blessed be the LORD, who hath not given us as a prey to their teeth. Our soul is escaped as a bird out of the snare of the fowlers: the snare is broken, and we are escaped. Our help is in the name of the LORD, who made heaven and earth."*

Can you recall all your shakings in the past years? It was God's mercies that kept you.

3.   God was teaching Jonah a lesson

Shakings are lessons of life. If you don't learn through experience, you will never grow. People who have substance to share and who became references are those who have been trained through the University of "Hard Knocks".

Paul said in Hebrews 5:15 _ *"But strong meat belongeth to them that are of full age, even those who by reason of use have their senses exercised to discern both good and evil"*

Shaking makes you full of age and your senses exercised. What makes you an elder or champion in the kingdom is not your age, but your experiences and walk with God.

It is your experience that determines your expression and manifestation.

4.   The fish was only obeying God's command

There is a limit every shaking will go. The instruction from God to the fish in my own word was: "swallow Jonah, but don't take his life!" Yes! God made the fish, and they will hear and obey Him.

God also spoke to Satan in the case of Job:

"And the LORD said unto Satan, Behold, all that he hath is in thy power; only upon himself put not forth thine hand. So Satan went forth from the presence of the LORD" -Job 1:12

God said, 'You can do anything to Job, but don't touch his life!'

Friends, that shaking you are going through will not crush you. You are in the hands of God as the clay is in the hands of the potter. God is bringing great things out of your life Halleluyah!

46

WHAT TO DO IN TIMES OF SHAKING

Since we now understand that God is involved in most of our shakings, we have no need to fear or panic. He will surely make a way of escape for His children.

1. Maintain your prayer life

When it seems hard to pray, that is the time to pray hard. Example is Daniel. A decree was passed because of him in the province that no one should pray to other God or gods except to king Dairus. But Daniel when he heard it, went to his house, opened the windows and prayed three times daily as he normally did (Daniel 6:10). God vindicated him at last when he was thrown into the lion's den. Let nothing stop you from praying. Even Jonah prayed in the fish belly. Keep up your prayer life.

2. Maintain your trust and confidence in God

Job, during the season of his shakings declared: "Though he slay me, yet will I trust in him: but I will maintain mine own ways before him" Job 13:15.

Keep trusting God. Hebrews 10:35-36 also tells us; "Cast not away therefore your confidence, which hath great recompense of reward. For ye have need of patience, that, after ye have done the will of God, ye might receive the promise"

God is so faithful and sure to bring you out to a place of rest after your shaking.

3. Maintain Your Integrity

This is where so many people failed God. The season of shaking is not the time to compromise your faith. The test of faith is to keep standing. So many ministers have gone into occultism because they couldn't press through in their shaking season. Some young ladies fell cheap to evil men. Joseph maintained his integrity while he was in Egypt. He was thrown into prison for false accusations, but he ended up as prime minister in Egypt.

## 4.	Maintain your confession

Keep declaring who God is to you and what He will do for you. The three Hebrew Children refused to bow to the image of Nebuchadbezzer. They declared that the God they served was able to deliver them from the fiery furnace (Daniel 3:16-18). The time of shaking is the time to keep confessing the word of faith.

## 5.	Maintain your dedication and passion

Don't stop your praying, giving, praising and services to God. I have seen people who grew cold during shakings. They stopped going to church. Continue what you were doing in greater proportion just like Daniel did when he prayed three times daily.

6. Maintain your life of praise and thanksgiving

Let nothing take the songs of Zion from your mouth. The children of Israel while in captivity hung their harps and musical instruments. They refused to sing further (Psalm 137). I like what Paul and Silas did while they were thrown into prison. They prayed and sang praises to God (Acts 16:25-26). Suddenly, there was Divine intervention. Jonah in the fish belly also gave a sacrifice of thanksgiving (Jonah 2:9).

The conclusion

"And the LORD spake unto the fish, and it vomited out Jonah upon the dry land" Jonah 2:10.

The same God that allowed the fish to swallow Jonah also spoke to the fish to vomit him. The

God that allowed shakings to come to you will speak to the source of the shaking to stop. Whatever is holding you down will hear the voice of God. You are coming out of every shaking in Jesus name.

God will give you wings to soar like the eagles. There shall be Divine Restoration in Jesus name!

52

THE BREAKING SEASON OF MINISTRY

Lets take a look at Luke chapter 5:1-7 and learn some lessons about the breaking seasons of life and ministry.

"And it came to pass, that, as the people pressed upon him to hear the word of God, he stood by the lake of Gennesaret, And saw two ships standing by the lake: but the fishermen were gone out of them, and were washing their nets. And he entered into one of the ships, which was Simon's, and prayed him that he would thrust out a little from the land. And he sat down, and taught the people out of the ship. Now when he had left speaking, he said unto Simon, Launch

out into the deep, and let down your nets for a draught. And Simon answering said unto him, Master, we have toiled all the night, and have taken nothing: nevertheless at thy word I will let down the net. And when they had this done, they enclosed a great multitude of fishes: and their net brake. And they beckoned unto their partners, which were in the other ship, that they should come and help them. And they came, and filled both the ships, so that they began to sink".

Peter laboured all night and caught nothing. There are people who laboured through years of ministry like peter. Thank God that Jesus stepped into the situation and helped him out. He was involved with them in their boat.

As long as you know that you have opened up for Christ to work through you, there is a season of blessings coming in all your labours.

After labouring, the word came to Peter to launch into the deep. It was a Rhema word. There is a word that you need to launch you to your next phase in ministry. The word came and there was an overflow. If there is anything any minister is praying for, it is overflow. It is result. When ministry begins to expand, it brings joy and gladness.

In the midst of the excitement, something happened.

a.   The Net broke! Vs 6.

There was a breaking at the height of breakthrough.

THEIR NET BROKE. What does it mean?
They were about losing it. They had laboured and caught nothing. Now they succeeded. They were loosing it

Breaking season is when things look tearing apart. Everyone with vision must have experienced the breaking seasons of life and ministry. When it seems you are settling down things suddenly began to break.

b.   The Boat Began to Sink.

Breaking can sink you if not properly handled. Some ministry can't handle the weight of success because they lack the necessary capacity.

What Sinks the Ship

a.   Heavy Burdens. The workload becoming too much.

b.   Pressure, Stress, fatigue, tiredness.

c.   Lack of Effective Management. When breakthrough comes, you need administrators

d.   Lack of Capacity. The net was not strong and big enough. When you have not built enough capacity to handle success, it can sink you.

Your success can reveal your capacity. Your challenges can also reveal your capacity.

Give someone with one thousand dollars capacity to handle a million dollars, in less than six month, the million will reduce to his level. But give someone else with one million dollar capacity to handle a thousand dollars; he will also increase it to his level.

So many of us might want to pastor the fifty thousand auditorium church of Canaan land, built by Living Faith church in Nigeria. If you are put there in just one month, you might have heart attack.... it will sink you.

Build capacity today, so that you will be able to manage breaking and breakthrough season when they come.

Things That Bring Shaking

1.   Partial Obedience.

Carrying out half instruction. For example: Peter was told to let down the nets (Plural) but he let down one net. Maybe you are not doing it right.

2.   The Fish.

They were tearing the net. The fishes are members. When ministry begins to grow, some members can cause break up. They are: stubborn members, bad Associates etc. They are all in the net, bur some will tear it.

What the Breaking Season Reveal

1.   You Cannot Do it on Your Own.

The reason some ministers break down at the breaking point is because they do things on their own. Lone rangers will never last in ministry. You can't handle the burden on your own.

2.   You Need a Network.

They called on their partners in the other ship to help them. You need me and I need you. Connect with people in other sip. You need partners. The only net that works is networking.

3.   *You Need Helpers.*

When things are breaking down you need divine helpers. Most people struggle because they lack helpers. If you deny your need for hep, you will break down. Jesus was there, but Peter still needs helpers. God will only do the supernatural but we need destiny helpers to support us.

4.   *Breaking tells You Your need to Move to the Next Level.*

Until you break out, you cannot stretch and reach out. Breaking expands you. So many of us are so comfortable at a particular place or location, God needs to break you to move you out.

5.   *Breaking Breaks You.*

It helps to shape your character. It humbles you. You need to see how proud some ministers are, it takes breaking to humble them.

6.   *Breaking Reveals the God Personality in You.*

It is at your breaking point that God brings out the real you that needs to get to the other side.

7.   *Breaking Releases the Bad Fishes to Go.*

When the net broke, some fishes swim out. There are some members that are not needed for the next level. They condition you for the net and cause trouble always. Let them go.

8.   *Breaking Creates Room for More.*

If your net doesn't break, you will not need more nets. So when the net breaks, more people you couldn't contain are coming.

After breaking comes explosion, expansion, and expression.

THE GREAT SHAKING

I have experienced several shakings in my journeys of life and ministry, but this shaking came as a bomb! It rocked and hit me so hard. It was the call to glory of my beloved wife, Pastor Nene Ibitoye. She was the wife of my youth, my sweetheart, inestimable jewel. May 15, 2020 will remain forever in my memory a history of the real unexpected and devastating news of the death of my sweetheart. We sat down together to edit this book you are reading from the first chapter as I wrote on the next phase of my assignment in ministry. There was a delay in completing the book due to the global locked down caused by covid-19 pandemic. South Africa was locked down in

Mach 2020 and we planned to complete and publish the book after the lock down. Little did I know that I will be writing this chapter in her memory.

The week of her transition to glory was filled with joy as she was at her best. She ministered on Facebook live stream on Mother's Day May 11, 2020. Her message that day was very inspiring. She brought a message of hope to her audience which is still fresh in our memories. The next day Monday 12th she sat with me praying at the background as I did my Winning Word live broadcast on Facebook . Tuesday 13th, we both ministered and prayed for people online at 12 midnight. On Wednesday, she sat at the background with me while I ministered again online. Then came that Thursday 15th, we were together at the sitting room with a guest. We ate and shared the word together. As soon as the guest left, she told me she had headache and needed to sleep for a while. Within an hour of her sleep, she woke up and began to vomit. I calmed her down and put a cold towel on her head so she can relax. She slept again and woke up at 2am vomiting, I then call for the ambulance. Before they came, she fainted on my arm. I quickly called one of my sons and we rushed her to the hospital. That was the last time I saw my wife alive – she passed on to glory.

HER BIOGRAPHY

Nene Ibitoye popularly known as Nene Eme prior to marriage was born into the family of Late Elder Eme Ogba Eme and Pastor Florence Enyidia Eme on the year of our Lord 1st October 1975 at the Island Maternity Lagos marking the independence of Nigeria. She was also popularly called Independence girl.

She is from Agbonta Amaugbagha Amaokwe Item Bendel LGA in Abia State, Nigeria. She began her childhood education in the defunct All Saint Nursery School in Ikorodu, Lagos, Nigeria before proceeding to Local Government Primary School where she was known for her reservedness and neatness and became a prefect. She attended Ipakodo Secondary School where she completed her Education in 1991. She gained admission into the University of Agriculture Abeokuta (UNAB) in Ogun State, Nigeria where she studied Biochemistry. She graduated and served her nation in Bayelsa State, Nigeria. After her trip to the United Kingdom, she got connected with Pastor Mike a multi-talented young preacher and this led to their marriage in 2004. She gave birth to Mojisola Ebubechukwu Ibitoye in June 20, 2005 and Damilola Onyinyechi on the 1st of January 2007 while her husband was far away in South Africa in 2007. She left Nigeria later in 2007 to join her husband in Cape Town where she finally gave birth to her son Olamide Akachukwu Ibitoye on 4th April 2009.

Pastor Nene Ibitoye was a very kind- and open-hearted woman which is usually accompanied by a resonating laugh or smile that hits the receiver with great warmth. She is the ideal virtuous woman spoken of in Proverbs 31, holding forte for her husband who travels wide every year leaving the church and family in her care. She is a great preacher of the word whose life and messages have blessed lives tremendously. She will be missed by her siblings, mum, church, husband, children, and everyone that have encountered her. We are however grateful to God for a life well lived in His presence and we are assured to meet her on the last day where we shall meet to part no more.

Rest in the bosom of the Father

Adieu Sister Adieu Daughter
From Siblings and Mum

HER PECULIARITIES

1.   A HOME BUILDER.
Pastor Nene is a home maker and builder. She was a perfect home organiser. I have no problem because she is there. She knew the

next thing to do when things are not in place. She made it very easy for me to travel to nations without worries about the home.

2.   A WOMAN OF FAITH.
Pastor Nene is not easily shaken. She lives by the principles of God's word. We have been through thick and thins together, but you will never see her frown her face at challenges. She often smiles and say, 'It is well'. Everyone knows her for that language. I am a preacher of faith, but she lives the faith more than me. I preach it, she lives it.

I remember when I was deported from South Africa to Nigeria in 2008, she told me to go home and she will hold on for me until I came back. I finally came back five months after. She really stood her ground in her prayers and encouragement for me until I stood on my feet again.

3. A TRUE PASTOR.

She is loved by the church for her simplicity and care. She preached faith and encouraged the people to stand firm on the word of God. I go on mission for weeks and even months and she pastored the church until I am back. I do not invite guest speakers when I travel, she is the pastor, coach, and speaker.

4. A MODEL.

Aside from spiritual qualities, pastor Nene is a very beautiful woman in and out. She is not loud in her dressing and make-up, but she knows how to combine what she has with simplicity and she comes out very admirable and attractive. I have no reason to look out to other women because she packaged herself very enough for me. She filled and occupied my space, she so loved me that she gives me the best of herself. She called me 'sweet'. She also worked with acting and modelling agencies. She is well sought after to play roles. Even few days after her death, I received message on her phone for a role that would have fetched her some good money.

5.   A MOTHER TO OUR CHILDREN.

She so loved our children and gave them the best both spiritually and mentally. Our children are always among the best learners in their school. they are always featured at the end of year award ceremony. She did her best to ensure that they achieved in their academics. The foundation she has laid for them will serve as a platform for them to excel in all areas of life.

TRIBUTES ON HER FUNERAL SERVICE

Apostle Mike Ibitoye (Husband)

To my Beloved Wife, Pastor Nene Ibitoye,

My sunshine, my sweetheart, the wife of my youth, the woman of inestimable value. Your passing away on May 15, 2020 at Grooteschurr hospital is still a very terrible shock. You were ecstatic and joyful during the last week and hours you spent with us, the period the children and I will forever remember and cherish in our hearts. Your laugher, smile, voice, the way you light up makes the home a very warm place. Your absence is irreplaceable.

The last charge you gave us on Mother's Day still resonates as if you knew we were about to go through an irreparable affliction. You spoke about the affliction we go through that people are aware of and God sees. You also went further to tell us of affliction that we can share with close friends, family members and spouses - I truly want to share this I feel with you now. You further reiterated that there are afflictions that you cannot share with anyone no matter how intimate, but God says He knows it all. In this I rest.

God in His infinite wisdom has divinely orchestrated your rapturous departure... though painful, we surrender to His will. Our wonderful family has been blessed by you with very evident proofs.

My dear Sweet as I always call you. You were not only a wonderful wife to me and mother to our loving children, you were a meticulous homemaker, cheerful, friendly, and you made many warm friends. You were Spirit filled following the guidance of the Spirit few days before you left, to call your fellow Pastor's wives, friends and family not knowing you were bidding them farewell as they were equally important to you.

Your great qualities and warm nature made you see the best in everyone even in impossible circumstances.

You loved the Lord, you loved the church, and you faithfully served which afforded me the opportunity to reach farther to the nations.

My dear Nene, my irreplaceable jewel, I miss you in a very unquantifiable way, and so does

Mojisola, Damilola, and Olamide... and so will everyone - the entire family, our friends present here and outside, and those watching online miss you sorely.

Words cannot describe what you meant to me. You inspired me in the sixteen years we were together, and you will continue to do so.

I am eternally grateful to God for the opportunity given me to be your husband, pastor, friend, companion, and confidant on this side of life.

In closing, my best friend, I want you to rest in the bosom of the Lord that you loved and served with all your heart.

Till we meet again, Rest in Perfect Peace.

Love from your husband,
Mike

Mojisola Ibitoye (Daughter)

My mother Nene Ibitoye the wife of Mike Ibitoye was the best mother one can have. She always encouraged me to do my work, to study when I am supposed to, to hand in my assignments early, etc. and because of her I am one of the tops in my grade. She had that beautiful smile of hers that gave me butterflies in my stomach. That smile of hers would always make me feel warm, comfortable, and safe. In every situation she always knew to trust in God because He knows everything, and He has a reason for everything. She always had that saying, 'it is well'. I miss those times we used to irritate her. You know sitting at home doing almost nothing gets boring sometimes so what me and my siblings used to do is that we used to irritate her just for the fun of it and that would bring so much joy to the house.

I have a poem for my mother:

A Mother's Love

A Mother's love is something
that no one can explain,
It is made of deep devotion
and of sacrifice and pain,
It is endless and unselfish
and enduring come what may
For nothing can destroy it
or take that love away . . .
It is patient and forgiving
when all others are forsaking,
And it never fails or falters
even though the heart is breaking . . .
It believes beyond believing
when the world around condemns,
And it glows with all the beauty
of the rarest, brightest gems . . .
It is far beyond defining,
it defies all explanation,
And it still remains a secret
like the mysteries of creation . . .

A many splendoured miracle
man cannot understand
And another wondrous evidence
of God's tender guiding hand.
(By Helen Steiner)

Rest in peace mum, till we meet again ay Jesus feet
Mojisola

Damilola Ibitoye (Daughter)

My mother was a very cheerful ad smiling person. She was the person who encouraged and pushed us to do our best. My mother was not only a parent to me, but also a friend. she always found a way to make me smile when I am down either by telling me a joke or by tickling me and that was the type of person she was. She always found a way of putting a smile on everyone's face. I still remembered those times we would wake up at 10am in the morning and she would call my name and laugh. My mum was the light of the house. She was a person who would just randomly stand up and dance. My mother was a positive speaker. She always said 'it is well' or 'God can do it' during hard times. My mum did not only encourage us, but my dad too when we are low spirited. My mums dream was to one day go to heaven and I am glad that dream became a reality. My mum was not only a blessing to us, but to everyone she came across. She will be missed dearly by her friends and family.

Mummy, may you rest in peace,

Damilola

Olamide Ibitoye (Son)

Mommy was the best mom ever; she would always take care of me when I am not feeling well. She was a very loving and kind mother and would always tell me my rights from my wrongs. She always took us to see beautiful places and would make sure we always had a

smile on our faces. She always had that saying, "It is well", that she used to in every situation, she never doubted God and knew that God would come through in everything and every situation. I am so sad that she had to leave the world so early, but I feel peace and warmth in my heart knowing that she is in a happy place, in heaven, with the Lord our father.
Rest in peace dear Mummy
I am Olamide

Pastor Rowina Stanley (Mentee)

As I tried to wrap my mind around what seemed to be a premature departure, the word "assignment" came to mind! And I was reminded that Pastor Nene's assignments in all its forms had come to an end...

I remember her as:
* A strong, warm, and friendly woman
* A never complained but contented
* A Good listener
* Passionate about God and His Word

* A true worshiper
* A Fiery preacher
* An intercessor
* A compassionate heart for women's issues
* A Genuine and sincere person

We are all on assignment

Our assignments as God's children are many, some small and some huge according to God's plan and purposes for our lives and span over long and short seasons. But they are all temporary and they all come to an end at God's appointed time. We very seldom know the exact time only God does. But God's grace is sufficient since His strength is perfected in our weakness!

But our assignments big and small, by God's grace should leave a mark for His Kingdom.

Pastor Nene had many assignments which came to an end on 15th May 2020 at God's appointed time.

What were these?

-       Her assignment as a wife and mother here on earth came to an end.

-       Her assignment as pastor and church leader here on earth came to an end.

-       Her assignment as a sister in Christ, mentor and friend here on earth came to an end.

-       Her assignment as an influencer here on earth came to an end.

And she did them all well to the best of her ability!

So, what is it that stood out for me in the past seven years that was incorporated in her assignments;

* The joy of the Lord was her strength!
* She persevered under her trials and challenges!
* She had the gift of contentment!

But her eternal assignment in heaven has just begun!

To be absent from the body is to be present with the Lord scripture teaches us in Psalm 116:15 – ***"Precious in the sight of the LORD is the death of His saints"***.

Pamela Naidoo   (Spiritual Daughter)

Tribute to My Risen Pastor, who fell asleep safe in the Arms of our Lord and Saviour on 15 May 2020.

Pastor Nene Ibitoye a loving wife to Apostle Mike, dear mother to Mojisola, Damilola and Olamide. My encouragement to us and to the family is God say to you today, He will wipe every tears from their eyes, and there will be no more death or sorrow, crying our pain, all these things are gone forever.

Today we grieve a beautiful soul who has taken rest, I Pam Naidoo on behalf of The

Winning Life Church and my Family met Pastor Nene 8 years ago. God said to us in In Jeremiah 3:15 that He would give us Pastor after his Own heart which will feed us with Knowledge and understanding. Pastor Nene has been a strong woman after God's heart. She has played a mother's role in my life, leading me, praying for me, the church, and my family. She had a heart after women, always encouraging and uplifting them. Pastor Nene was a mother to many.

She has left imprints in my life that I will treasure forever. If you knew her then you would know that she was always smiling and never shaken, always declaring God's words. She taught me to say, 'It is well'. Through it all standing alongside and supporting Apostle Mike in his calling and ministry and being a pastor is never an easy calling, but she never got tired. She never complained and would just smile.

To me it was truly an honour and privilege to have crossed paths with you Pastor Nene., always devoted and giving so much, only God knows all the Souls she touched.

This is not goodbye my spiritual mum, sister, and friend, but rather good night. Rest well until that Glorious Day when we shall meet again.

Love You Always and will miss you.

Pam Naidoo.

LESSONS I LEARNT FROM HER DEATH

1.   *Live Prepared.*

Life is a mystery, only God has the interpretation. Pastor Nene had a glorious week full of joy and excitement as if she knew she was going home to the Father. Few days before her death, she told me she had a leading by the Spirit to call Women ministers and wives to encourage them in the Lord. Her call to them surprised them. I overheard one of the pastors asking her if there was any problem that prompted her call. She also called her siblings and mum as well. More so, we took family photos after her online preaching on Mother's Day which we have not done for a very long time. She took a personal picture and changed her profile picture on Facebook as well. When I looked at her after that, I was wandering if this was Pastor Nene I married – she was looking so radiant and beautiful. We never knew she will leave us that same week.

This is a major lesson I learnt through her death. We must live our lives daily pleasing the Lord as if that will be our last day on earth. We sat down together that morning, ate together with a guest, and them few hours later, she was gone. I see it as her own rapture. Jesus will either come suddenly to take us home, or we will go to meet him though death. Live prepared.

2.   *Give Yourself to a Cause*

She fulfilled her purpose in life. Her life may have been short-lived, but she lived it for a cause. Your donation to life supersedes your duration in life. Jesus lived for thirty-three and half years, but his impact is still speaking. It is better to live a life of impact than to barely live without fulfilling God's purpose for your life.

3.   *God is Sovereign.*

We are all living by the mercies of God. We do not have the final say to life, do your best and leave the rest to God. I question God why He allowed my wife to die, but the truth of the matter is that who am I to question Him? He knew it will happen and He allowed it despite all our prayers. It does not matter how holy we live, how powerful we pray, or how many scriptures we know, God still has the final say when it comes to matters that pertains to life.

4.   *Endeavour to move on no matter your pains*

It is painful to lose a loved one, but we must allow ourselves to be healed and move on with life. There are more territories to conquer and possess. Pastor Nene and I had great plans of things to do and achieve. She will be so disappointed in heaven to see me stopped because of the grief of her departure. I believe she is interceding on my behalf in heaven and watching over our children too. Just like Abraham buried his dead (Sarah) out of his sight in Genesis 23:1-20, I have buried my dead so I can see farther and further to move on with the journeys of life and ministry.

INSPIRATIONAL POEMS FROM MY HEART

This life called LIFE

No one has the interpretation except God.
No one knows the depth, height, width, except God.

1 Cor 13:9 "For we know in part, and we prophesy in part"

This life called LIFE is lived in part.
We play our part.
We do our part
Our part is the portion assigned for us
This life called life is full of mysteries
The secrets you do not know belong to God
The secret you know is what is revealed to you.
What you can see is what is allowed.

This life called LIFE is a question.
It is one of the most profound questions of human existence, and virtually no one knows the answer...
or if an answer even exists at all: "What is the meaning of life?" The answer will transform your life

This life called LIFE is a search.
We live to search out matters... We find, we gain, we lose, we let go...

This life called LIFE is a gift from God.
Accept it, appreciate it, cherish it, do your best...
You may not know the value... until you lose it
Do your best and leave the rest to God

This life called LIFE is something we will understand better
This life called LIFE is summarised in ONE WORD

"So then it is not of him that willeth, nor of him that runneth, but of God that sheweth mercy" Roman 9:16

MERCY... is the interpretation of this life called LIFE

PAUSE... PAUSED...

That word is constant...

At times we pause ... at times we are paused.
We pause to reflect, think, and concentrate.

Sometimes we are paused by things we cannot handle.,.

Pausing is not the end of the journey...

To pause is to wait...
When the music plays and we want to get the lyrics...the rhythm, the meaning... the message... we must Pause...

There are still lots to learn and to know after the pause...

You can pause at the beginning... the middle... or at the end... But pausing is not the end...

It is in our pause that God speaks ...

Moses paused.

"And the angel of the LORD appeared unto him in a flame of fire out of the midst of a bush: and he looked, and, behold, the bush burned with fire, and the bush was not

consumed. And Moses said, I will now turn aside, and see this great sight, why the bush is not burnt" Exd 3:2-3

When the fire burns... turn aside for details.
God speaks when you pause...

"And when the LORD saw that he turned aside to see, God called unto him out of the midst of the bush, and said, Moses, Moses. And he said, Here am I" Exd 3:4

When you pause... and when you are paused...
God has SOMETHING TO SAY....

Pray with me:
"Oh Lord in my pause... and when I am paused... speak to me like Moses. 'Here am I'

COLOURS OF LIFE

Life is full of Colours...
Every day we paint just a little bit more,
each brush stroke bringing a blush of colour.

Red to represent the love we feel.
Blue for the sorrow that weaves through our lives, a river of ribbon.
Green for the new life that springs up like growth after a wildfire.
Here, a quick dash of orange, the stolen minutes between breaths where we can just stop.
Black... for isolation when we feel too alone to even think...
And the purple calm of an evening that comes after a long day.

We never know which colour will come next, but we will keep painting until the colours run dry

- Isiri Blackthorne

"Without black, no colour has any depth. But if you mix black with everything, suddenly there's shadow – no, not just shadow, but fullness. You've got to be willing to mix black

---

into your palette if you want to create something that's real."

Ephesians 5:15-16 tells us:
"Be very careful, then, how you live — not as unwise but as wise, making the most of every opportunity, because the days are evil."

Take advantage of new opportunities daily to strengthen your faith and paint meaningful colours in your everyday life...

Each day is a colour to paint

Pastor Nene Ibitoye will forever live in our hearts.

Now comes the shift!

THE COVID-19 PANDEMIC SHAKING

The entire world was hit with the invasion of Covid-19 pandemic. Never in history has there been such shakings that it affected the religious, political, social, and financial systems. The deaths recorded were much, just as the first and second world war claimed lives. Can we say this is the third world war by pandemic?

There are several controversies rising as to the purpose of this pandemic. Some believed there are hidden agendas otherwise called 'conspiracy theory'. Some others said it is a battle of supremacy between the world power especially USA and China. Other notions states that it is the effect of 5G radiations that is killing multitude of people, therefore, corona virus was developed as a cover up to kill people while the world powers are busy installing their 5G mask all over the nations. Some religious sectors believed that it was an end time agenda to usher in the antichrist as he will use the available technological means to rule the world. They believed that the coming of Jesus Christ is at hand. Whatever the case may be, the world will never forget Covid-19. Generations unborn will be told the story.

The effect of this pandemic was so devastating. The world was busy looking for solutions, but to no avail. The death toll over China, Europe, United Kingdom, USA was too alarming. Hospitals could not accommodate more infected people for lack of space, so more hospitals had to be built. The entire world lived in fear of infections and deaths. Nations had to close their borders to tourism and business. Every state, communities, streets, were locked down and no movements allowed. The order everywhere was, social distancing, washing of hands with hand sanitizers, covering of face and mouth with face masks. To make matters worse, religious worship centres were closed totally to avoid the spread of the virus. The fear of corona virus became the beginning of wisdom.

Covid-19 was a major shaking globally. At the beginning of the year 2020, no one envisaged that there will be an invasion of this pandemic. Things were going on as normal until the centre could no longer hold. There were lots of tourists and travellers that were locked down in various countries and were stranded because of the closure of international borders.

While people were feeling the effect of this pandemic, there were some that profited from it. What was devastating to others was profiting to some.

I believe the Covid -19 pandemic is one of the fulfilments of the end time prophecies according the scriptures. God said in the book of Haggai 2:6-7

".... Yet once, it is a little while, and I will shake the heavens, and the earth, and the sea, and the dry land; And I will shake all nations, and the desire of all nations shall come: and I will fill this house with glory, saith the LORD of hosts."

This present shaking may be artificial as the hands of men were involved in it, but there is no other way to describe it than to conclude that this is allowed by God.

Let us look at some of the effects of Covid -19 on the church.

1.   The desires of all nations are now redirected to God. Men became lovers of themselves instead of God but when this shaking came, they had to look up to God in prayers for solution.

2. **It has enabled the church to take advantage of the technological advancements to reach out to the world.** The physical building was closed, but the church did not close. The church is not the building, but the people otherwise known as the Body of Christ. Previously, so many preachers preached against social media and they criticized those using it. Social media has its own disadvantage too, but the advantage far outweighed it. Personally, it has enhanced my ministry outreach as I now reach out and build lots of followers. The church of this present times is the church that must operate beyond borders and limit. Virtual online meetings has become a tool globally of bringing people together at one time for meetings and engagements.

3. **It negatively affected faith in God.** The church could not stand on their faith

confession. We read of people like John G. Lake whose ministry brought healing to the sick during a pandemic in South Africa. The facemask closed the mouth of the church spiritually. Isaiah 60:1 says

"Arise, shine; for your light is come, and the glory of the Lord is risen upon you".

The church should shine amid this gross darkness.

The Covid 19 pandemic is like a rehearsal of the tribulation that awaits the world which was spoken of by Daniel the Prophet and by Jesus Christ. It is like the plague God brought to Egypt that destroyed the people. If just one plague was so devastating, just imagine the ten plague God brought to Egypt by the hands of Moses

We must understand vividly that we are in the end of times, and God is about to wrap up this dispensation of Grace. Present events and happenings are pointers to the church that Jesus Christ is coming again. If the church is not sensitive to the present truth, she will be lost while engaging with activities because of lack of knowledge.

We need people that will be sensitive to God's programme like the children of Issachar who understood the times, and their brethren were under their command (1 Chro. 12:32). The corona virus may have shaken the entire world system, but it has enabled people to shift in mindset, operation, and relationships.

The entire shakings of this present times are meant to shift humanity globally to a new dimension of operations. We must understand at this junction that the shifting has begun. We can no longer operate the ways we are used to, but we must navigate with times.

The shifting is here now. Are you ready to maximize it to move to the next phase?
See you on top.

OTHER BOOKS BY APOSTLE MIKE IBITOYE

FAITH BEYOND LIMITATIONS

Many Christians today are faced with limitations in their lives which ultimately prevents them from achieving God's purpose for their lives. In the situations we find ourselves, Christians are experiencing more fears, anxiety, and hopelessness that ever. Astronomical job layoffs, division in families, crime, and soaring suicidal statistics are recorded around the world, which forces people to ask for something more. Questions like, what can I do? How can I survive? Why is this happening to me? The reason Mike Ibitoye wrote this book is to provide answers to these questions

Faith beyond limitations will propel you the reader into a deeper understanding of faith. It contains powerful nuggets that will empower you to live above all kinds of limitations and enable you to fulfil your God-ordained purpose.

WINNING IN THE GAME OF LIFE

Laws and principles govern every game. The laws that govern football do not govern handball. Therefore, in the game of life, there are laws and principles you apply to win. In this book, Mike Ibitoye will teach you biblical keys to stardom. You will be empowered to dare every circumstance to become a celebrity. In its written pages, you will discover that the only place where things remain impossible is in your own thinking.

MAKING YOUR DREAMS A REALITY

Living without a dream results in doom! We live in a dreamer's world; only committed and active dreamers will make a mark in the sands of life. Dreams are the cure for tears; the car you drive, the house you live in, and everything around you are people's dreams.

In this book, Mike Ibitoye will teach you the power and the force of dreams and how you can birth yours. You will learn how to:

- Turn your dreams to reality
- Start with what you have
- Overcome the fear of failure
- Be successful inside out
- Handle the weight of success

You will be challenged to harness the gift of God in you and maximize it for great productivity.

TAKING YOUR PLACE IN DESTINY

There are people whose destinies are designed and meant for the top, but where they are right now is just a state of despair. When you are out of place in life, you are misplaced, and can be replaced.

To be begging when you are supposed to be giving to others is an evil. Also, to be qualified in life with great potentials and credentials and remain under servitude is an error. How can servants ride on horses while princes are walking? Beloved, it is foolishness!

In this book, Mike Ibitoye will unfold the miseries of life, and challenge you to take hold of your rightful position. It is the mysteries of the kingdom that will help you to gain mastery over the miseries of life.

THE SECRETS OF OPEN HEAVENS

Have you ever wondered why people, despite their qualifications, potentials, connections, and positions still struggle to make it in life? It is because heaven is closed against them. Anyone operating under closed heaven will never make will never make headway in a competitive society. When your heaven is opened, your earth will naturally release your needed blessings. In this book, you will discover how to:

- Access divine secrets to walk in open heavens
- Provoke God to step into your affairs
- Break free from limitations to possibilities
- Enjoy the best that life has to offer
- Leave the lower level and operate in a higher dimensional life

Packaged in this book are revealed truths that will bring spiritual revolution for you to take your place in life and rise from obscurity to limelight.

Get to Know
WINNING IN LIFE
INTERNATIONAL

We are an apostolic ministry committed to motivating, equipping, and releasing lives into their destinies in Christ.

Mode of Operations

1. Winning in Life Conference / Seminar
A faith motivational programme packaged to touch lives

2. Winning in Life Media Network
Broadcasting information that guarantees your transformation.

3. Winning in Life Publications
Publishing the word, lightening up the Nations through Books, Winning Word Today devotionals, Today's Winning Keys, and Winning Word for Ministers.

4. Mission to Nations

Touching Nations for Christ, fulfilling the scriptures "Go he into all the world.." Mk 16:15

5. Winning in Life School of Ministry

Raising, impacting, and releasing ministry gifts to the Body of Christ.

6. Winning in Life Bible Training Centre

Raising Champions that will touch their world

7. International Winning Summit

This is a gathering of leaders from nations to network, fellowship, and be imparted to enhance their productivity in life and ministry.

Winning in Life International Ministries is a network of ministers in the fivefold networking together and reaching out to nations at all cost with programs that will build the Body of Christ and expand the kingdom of God.

We have been in operation since 2001. You can connect with the grace of this ministry today.

Partnership

Connect with Apostle Mike Ibitoye with a team of ministers to reach the Nations for Jesus Christ.

Psalm 68:11 says ***"The Lord gave the word: great was the company of those that published it"***

You can be among the company of publishers. To sponsor any of our conferences in the nation, call or WhatsApp: +27789787816. This is a door you can trust for your next level in life and ministry

<u>Ministry Booking</u>

To Invite The Author To Speak At A
Conference, A Local Church or City/Nation,
Please Contact him at:

Apostle Mike O. Ibitoye
WINNING IN LIFE INTERNATIONAL MINISTRIES
Tel: +27 (0) 78 978 7816 (South Africa).
E-mail: michaelibitoye@gmail.com
Website: winninginlifeint.co.za